CONTENTS

The route card inside contains the route maps and information about the routes, waymarking, and transport, together with some walking advice.

To the best of our knowledge the historical content and all other information is believed to be correct. We should be grateful if you would inform us of any changes, omissions or errors, so that modifications can be made in subsequent revisions of the book.

INTRODUCTION

The Brockhill walks are the second in a series of circular walk networks linked to the Saxon Shore Way. In series with the Shorne and Higham Marshes walks. Other routes are planned and in preparation.

In response to public demand this publication is a combined guidebook and route card. It may be used intact or seperately by removing the waterproof route card carefully from the centre of the book. Whilst the guidebook contains background information about the area and other useful information, the route card is self-contained and can be used on the walk independently of the guidebook.

SAXON SHORE WAY

The Brockhill walks link with part of the Saxon Shore Way, a long distance route which traces the old shore line from Gravesend on the Thames estuary to Rye on the Kent-Sussex border. The name 'Saxon Shore' comes from a series of fortifications built by the Romans, mainly in the late fourth century, to defend the country against raids by Saxon pirates in the English Channel and the North Sea areas.

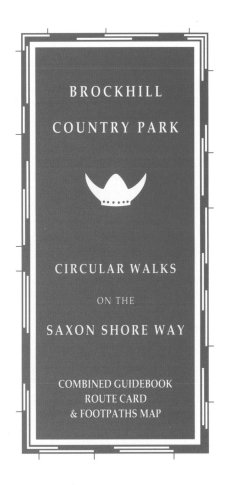

BROCKHILL

COUNTRY PARK

CIRCULAR WALKS

ON THE

SAXON SHORE WAY

COMBINED GUIDEBOOK
ROUTE CARD
& FOOTPATHS MAP

WELCOME TO THE GARDEN OF ENGLAND

Designed and produced by Countryside Group ,
Kent County Council, Planning Department,
and The Design Studio.

Maps produced by The Design Studio
with the sanction of the Controller of
HM Stationery Office.
Crown Copyright reserved.

Printed in Great Britain by
Springfield Litho, Sevenoaks, Kent.

Published by Kent County Council,
Planning Department, Springfield, Maidstone,
Kent, ME14 2LX.

First published March 1994.

Copyright© 1994 Kent County Council

ISBN 1 873010 37 0

Situated at the mouths of the main rivers, these forts contained troops and a fleet to give chase to the marauders and provided a frontier between the civilised and the barbarian world. The Saxon Shore Way passes four of these old forts along the way, Reculver, Richborough, Dover and Lympne, as well as many other places of historic interest, including Rochester and Sandwich. While the coastline has receded in several places,you find estuary and sea views for much of the way. The entire footpath runs for 140 miles.

NATURAL HISTORY

This series of routes passes through or near to a rich variety of wildlife habitats, including the grassland of the chalk downs, woodlands on the Gault Clay and Lower Greensand and the wetland habitats associated with the Royal Military Canal.

The route between Hythe and West Hythe follows the Royal Military Canal (8). Away from the urban area the canal becomes increasingly rich in aquatic and marginal vegetation with associated insects and other animals. Fringed water lily is a feature of the canal. Marsh frogs are plentiful, grass snakes breed here and so too does the increasingly uncommon common toad. Toads are creatures of habit, always returning to the same breeding site. Sadly, many are killed each year crossing the main road to reach the canal.

In summer you can see many different species of dragonfly and damselfly darting over the water including the emperor and brown aeshna dragonflies and the common blue damselfly. These colourful insects spend most of their lives, several years in some cases, in

their larval stage underwater. In summer look for emerging adults on the stems of waterside plants. Birds to look out for along the canal include heron, kingfisher and yellow wagtail.

COWSLIP

To the north of this section of the canal is a steep escarpment of Kentish ragstone. The ragstone, a sandy limestone, is associated with the Hythe Beds and forms part of the Lower Greensand formation. The grasslands and woodlands found on the calcareous soils of the escarpment are among the best remaining examples of semi-natural habitats on ragstone in Kent. As a result the area is designated as a Site of Special Scientific Interest (SSSI) by the Government's conservation body English Nature.

Lympne Park Wood(4) is a remnant of ancient woodland and is the largest remaining area of ash coppice woodland on the ragstone escarpment. The wood also includes oak, field maple and hazel. You may see some elm here but most mature specimens have succumbed to Dutch elm disease. The calcareous soils of Lympne Park Wood are also ideally suited to wayfaring-tree, spindle and privet. Woodland flowers include early purple and common spotted orchids.

Coppicing was once a widespread form of woodland management in Kent and some woodlands are still managed in this way. The trees are cut to ground level on a regular cycle and allowed to regrow. The multiple stems are then cut for fencing, tools, firewood and a variety of other uses. Coppicing increases the light reaching the woodland floor encouraging a carpet of flowers in the spring. This, together with the rich mosaic of habitats associated with coppiced woodland results in a tremendous variety of wildlife living in and using the wood.

On the grasslands of the escarpment, grasses include cock's foot, false oat grass and a variety of fescues. Cowslip, carline thistle and hound's tongue grow in the open areas. The mild humid conditions of this south-facing slope, so close to the sea, encourage a wealth of mosses and ferns. The high humidity allows plants normally associated with woodlands to survive in the open grassland including wood sedge and stinking iris.

East of Lympne, the path passes the edge of Folks Wood(7). The geology here is Gault Clay and the presence of heavy clay soils makes this coppiced woodland very wet. Sweet chestnut, hornbeam and ash grow in the wood and the presence of plants such as lesser skullcap and betony indicates that this wood is of ancient origin.

East of Pedlinge is Brockhill County Park(11). Here a deep ravine cuts through the Lower Greensand. The ravine is wooded with alder and oak along the stream and floodplain. Beech and oak high forest grows on the drier ground of the ravine sides. Mature oak and ash are scattered throughout the grassland areas above the ravine. An ornamental lake and the presence of exotic tree species such as walnut, date back to when the area was once part of a large estate. Ferns are a feature here. Look out for hart's tongue fern, soft shield fern and polypody. The latter grows as an epiphyte on oak branches. Lichens grow in profusion with over 50 species recorded. Birds are numerous in the park and include great spotted and green woodpecker, nuthatch and treecreeper.

North of the A20 the path reaches the chalk escarpment with large areas of grassland. This open downland is a mass of wildflowers in summer including rock rose, squinancywort, thyme, cowslip and small scabious. Grazing by livestock and rabbits is essential to the survival of these species as it maintains the open character of the downland. Without grazing the grassland is slowly invaded by scrub vegetation such as hawthorn. This in turn is ultimately succeeded by woodland.

North of Postling village the path passes through a very good example of chalk downland habitat (Postling Down 16) rich in grasses and other wildflowers. Grasses include sheep's and red fescue, oat grass, quaking grass and crested hair grass. Flowers include bird's-foot-trefoil, horseshoe vetch, the larval foodplant of the Adonis blue butterfly, small scabious and a number of orchid species including common spotted and bee orchid. In summer the grasslands are alive with the sight and sounds of bees, butterflies, crickets and grasshoppers. Two of the more uncommon butterflies here are the tiny grizzled and dingy skippers. Skylark and kestrel often fly overhead and you may see runs of the field vole and other small mammals in the longer grass.

At Tolsford Hill(18) light gravelly soils are found in an area of tumulii. Here the chalkland flora is replaced by acid grass and heath with heather, sheep's sorrel and mosses.

Between Tolsford Hill and Saltwood, the path passes some small remnants of ancient woodland. These areas of damp, mixed broadleaved woodland have been actively coppiced in the past. Trees here include ash, oak and hornbeam. Woodland flowers growing here include the very attractive lady orchid, greater butterfly orchid, herb Paris and stinking iris. In very damp areas species such as ragged robin, opposite-leaved saxifrage and pendulous sedge can be seen.

INTERESTING FEATURES

1 Studfall Castle
In Roman times the sea reached right up to the foot of the escarpment. The castle was built to guard the Roman port of Lemanis (Portus Lemanis), which was at the southern end of Stone Street, the Roman road that led straight to Durovernum, which we now call Canterbury.

Much of the cliff area here had been made unstable by the action of the sea at the bottom. This is most dramatically shown by the ruined walls of the castle which was built in the late 3rd century AD. Some time in the early medieval period the whole cliff, on which the castle was built, slid down into the silted harbour below. The old walls lie in the sloping fields between the ridge of the escarpment and the Royal Military Canal below.

Excavations here in the mid-19th century, and in the early 1980s, have found the sites of the main gates on the east and west, and shown that the Roman garrison probably left the castle in the mid-4th century AD.

2 Lympne Castle

This castle belonged to the Archdeacons of Canterbury from soon after the Norman Conquest, when it was first built, until the 19th century. It was another of the defences of the south-east in the Middle Ages, and at the core of the present group of buildings (restored and greatly added to at the beginning of this century) are a fine late-14th-century great hall, porch, kitchen and chambers. There was a Roman watchtower in the walls in which a Roman shoe was found during restoration work.

BROCKHILL

COUNTRY PARK

CIRCULAR WALKS

ON THE

SAXON SHORE WAY

ROUTE CARD
& FOOTPATHS MAP

Kent County Council
COUNTRYSIDE

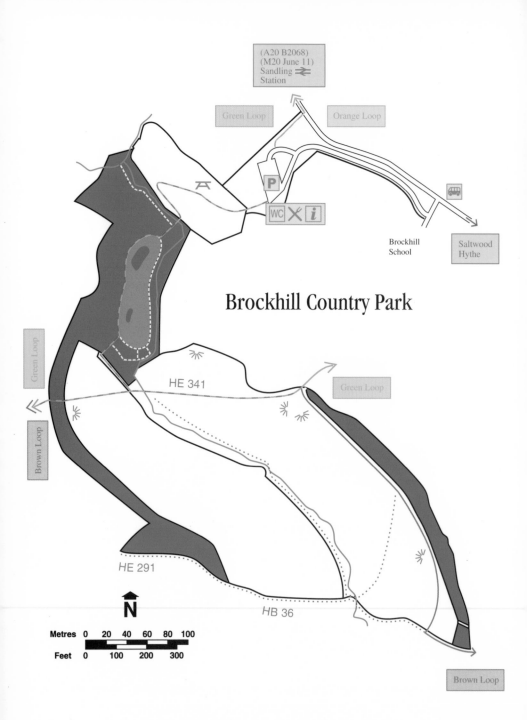

(A20 B2068)
(M20 June 11)
Sandling
Station

Green Loop

Orange Loop

P

WC

Brockhill
School

Saltwood
Hythe

Brockhill Country Park

Green Loop

Green Loop

HE 341

Brown Loop

HE 291

HE 291

HB 36

Brown Loop

N

Metres 0 20 40 60 80 100

Feet 0 100 200 300

THE ROUTES

The circular walks, which comprise loops ranging between 3 $^1/_2$ and 6 $^1/_2$ miles each, can be combined in any way to provide longer walks of up to 16 miles.

ROUTE MAP INFORMATION

The route maps are reproduced from the Ordnance Survey Pathfinder Series enlarged to a scale of 3 $^1/_2$" to the mile.

The maps are aligned north/south on both pages. For convenience, the north point and scale appears on the maps.

Maps

Ordnance Survey sheet numbers and titles:

Landranger Series, scale 1:50,000 - 1 $^1/_4$" to 1 mile.
179 Canterbury & East Kent area.

Pathfinder Series, scale 1:25,000 - 2 $^1/_2$" to 1 mile.
1252 (TR13/23) Folkestone and Hythe.

Distances and Times

The distances and times for each loop are shown on the maps.

WAYMARKING

The circular walks are colour coded and the background colours of the waymark arrows correspond to the colours of the routes on the maps. The waymarks are fixed to poles and posts of gates or stiles, or routed into waymark posts.

The walks have been waymarked in such a way that is possible for you to walk the routes in either direction; the waymarks face both directions.

TRANSPORT

Car Parking

Car parking places are shown on the route maps. Please note that these are not necessarily car parks. If a car park is not available, please park thoughtfully and sensibly to avoid causing an obstruction or damage to the roadside verges. Leave your car securely locked with valuables out of sight.

Bus Service

A bus service operates between Canterbury and Hythe on Monday to Saturday at a two-hour frequency. For details contact Kent County Council, Highways and Transport action Department, Springfield, Maidstone, Kent ME14 2LX, telephone Maidstone (0622) 696996.

Train Service

A train service to Sandling Station operates between Ashford and Folkestone seven days a week at an hourly frequency. For details, telephone either Tonbridge (0732) 770111 or London (071-928) 5100.

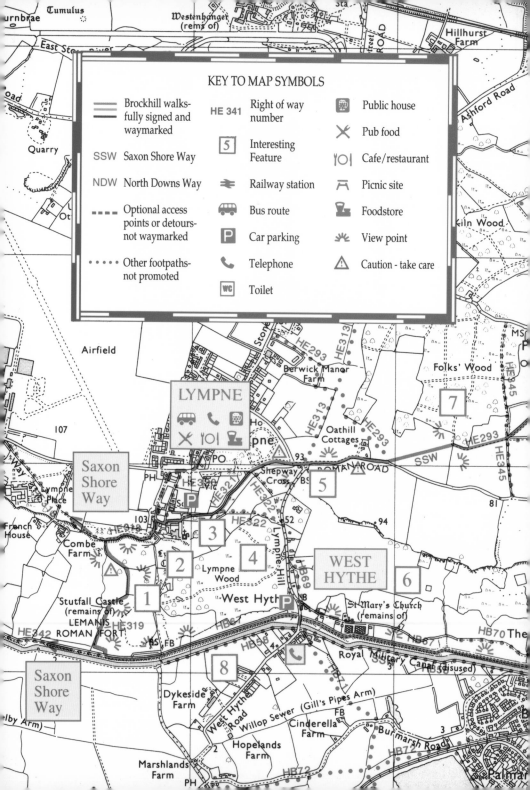

KEY TO MAP SYMBOLS

═══ Brockhill walks- fully signed and waymarked	HE 341 Right of way number	🍺 Public house
SSW Saxon Shore Way	5 Interesting Feature	✕ Pub food
NDW North Downs Way	⇥ Railway station	⦿l Cafe/restaurant
---- Optional access points or detours- not waymarked	🚌 Bus route	⊓ Picnic site
····· Other footpaths- not promoted	P Car parking	⬗ Foodstore
	☎ Telephone	✸ View point
	wc Toilet	⚠ Caution - take care

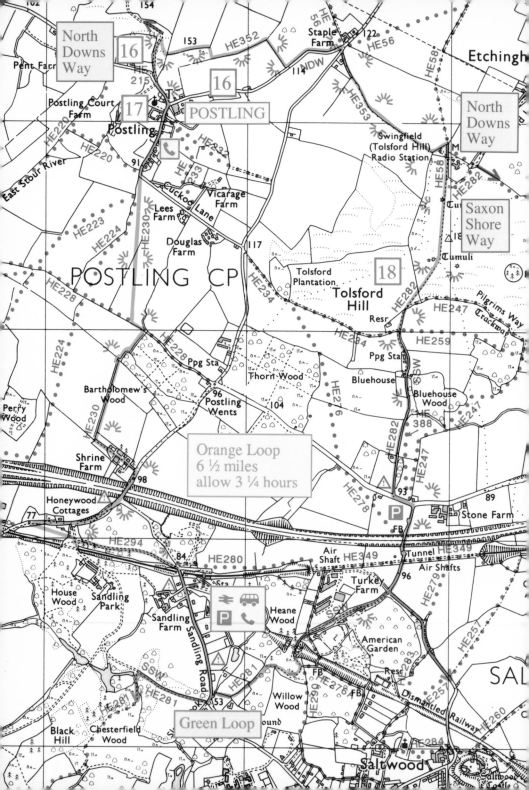

INTERESTING FEATURES
(for descriptions, see guidebook section)

1 Stutfall Castle

2 Lympne Castle

3 Lympne Church

4 Lympne Park Wood

5 Shepway Cross

6 West Hythe Church

7 Folks Wood

8 Royal Military Canal

9 Romney, Hythe and Dymchurch Railway

10 Chesterfield Wood

11 Brockhill Country Park

12 Willow Wood

13 Saltwood Rectory and American Garden

14 Saltwood Church

15 Saltwood Castle

16 Postling Down

17 Postling Church

18 Tolsford Hill

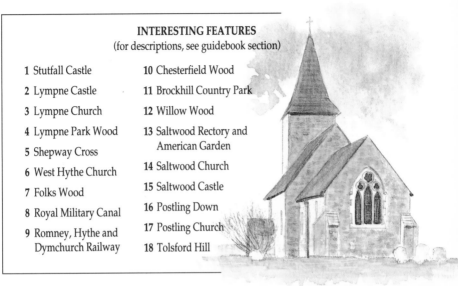

A WALKERS CODE

Remember that most of the public paths cross private estates and farmland. You are walking through a place of work; enjoy the countryside but please show respect for its life and work.

Always keep to the path to avoid trespass, but when faced with growing crops you may have to seek a way round the edge of the field. Otherwise walk in single file through a crop.

Remember to leave things as they are - fasten those gates you find closed. Straying stock can cause damage, and inconvenience to farmers. Always use gates and stiles to cross fences and hedges.

Take your litter home with you otherwise it can injure people and animals (including wildlife). Guard against all risk of fire, especially in dry weather. Picnicking is not permitted on private land; you only have a right of passage on a right of way.

To avoid injury or distress to farm animals and wildlife, keep your dogs under control at all times. If not on a lead they can run surprisingly long distances and consequently out of sight of the owner. Farmers have a right to shoot dogs found worrying animals.

Take care when crossing or walking along country roads. Keep to the right in single file facing oncoming traffic. On a bend, however, walk on the outside.

Always wear suitable clothing and footwear for the season. Be prepared for cold and wet weather, in which case take with you clothes which are warm and waterproof. Inexpensive overtrousers will protect you from any discomfort caused by walking through high vegetation or crops after rain. Sections of the path may be muddy after periods of rain so wear strong, comfortable and waterproof footwear.

Allow plenty of time to complete your chosen walk. Reckon on walking 2 to 2 $^1/_2$ miles an hour. Allow more time if it has been wet, if you are elderly or have children or inexperienced walkers with you.

3 Lympne Church

Immediately to the east of Lympne Castle is the fine parish church of St Stephen which has an early 12th-century crossing tower. This was originally a west tower with the nave to the east and a chancel beyond that. When the church was rebuilt in the 13th century, a new chancel was built on the site of the old nave, and a new nave was added west of the tower. A north chapel was also built at this time, as well as a small north aisle. The latter was enlarged in the early 14th century when the porch was built.

4 Lympne Park Wood

(See Natural History Section)

5 Shepway Cross

This was an important meeting place in the Middle Ages and gave its name to the whole district or Lathe, as it was called. (It is now the centre of the modern Shepway district).

At this point the main Roman road from Canterbury (Stone Street) descended the cliff to run to the Roman fort at Stutfall castle (through the later medieval deer park of the archdeacons, still an ancient wood, called Lympne Park Wood). The name Shepway almost certainly indicates a major track for sheep being brought up from Romney Marsh in the Anglo-Saxon period.

LYMPNE CASTLE

The cross marks the location of the original Court of the Cinque Ports - the Court of Shepway. It was a one-day court and sentences were meted out and literally executed on the spot; if a felon was sentenced to death he was drawn round the lathe of Shepway and publicly hanged.

At the top of Lympne Hill, the cross commands a fine view over Romney Marsh, Dungeness, Fairlight Hills and, on a clear day, even to the South Downs.

6 West Hythe Church

This ruined church was first built in the late 11th century and enlarged in the 13th century. It is at the extreme west end of the large medieval town of Hythe. This town is unusual since it constantly had to move eastwards because the shingle to the south gradually moved north-eastwards and blocked the large natural harbour at the mouth of the River Limen. The harbour was finally completely blocked in the 16th century, and the town shrunk to a small core below St Leonard's church. The rifle ranges are now situated on the shingle that fill the old harbour.

7 Folks Wood

(See Natural History Section)

8 Royal Military Canal

This defensive canal between Seabrook and Cliff End in Sussex, 28 miles long, was built

SHEPWAY CROSS

because of the fear of invasion by the French during the Napoleonic Wars. The canal was 44ft wide at the bottom, 62ft wide at the water's surface and 9ft deep. It had a defensive parapet all along its northern bank, made from the soil dug out to make the canal. It was finished in 1809, and is deliberately made in short offset lengths so that the defenders could fire down each section of the canal. A military road ran all along the northern bank.

It was also used as a conventional canal, and now provides angling, boating and a pleasant tree-lined walk.

Much of this section of the canal lies at the base of a series of landslips known as the Roughs. In this area Kentish ragstone was quarried in the Middle Ages.

9 Romney, Hythe and Dymchurch Railway

The world's smallest public railway line which runs for 14 miles on 15 inch tracks between Hythe and Dungeness, was the original idea of two racing drivers, Captain J Howey and Count Zborowski. The Count was tragically killed in a motor racing accident in Italy which left the Captain to continue alone with the scheme. The Southern Railway Company eventually offered a site on the Romney Marshes, with a view to expanding their own holiday business. The line was completed and operational by 1929. The miniature steam engines pull a selection of carriages and assorted rolling stock.

10 Chesterfield Wood

At the southern end of the wood are some very old Hazel stools on a bank that was once an ancient boundary. Further in, Hazel can be

seen again, this time as a coppice. Coppicing is an old forestry technique of cutting trees to ground level to produce fresh shoots which grow quickly from well established roots. The poles can be harvested after 5 to 20 years and are used for making hurdles, walking sticks and hop poles. Large oaks grow amongst the coppice as an over-storey and provide a very rich habitat for birds. In early summer the ground is a carpet of campion and bluebells.

11 Brockhill Country Park

Brockhill Country Park is situated on what was once part of the estate of Brockhill Park. The recorded history of the estate dates back to Norman times. A connection with the death of Thomas à Becket seems likely since his murderers had set out from nearby Saltwood Castle, the seat of 'one of the wickedest men in Christendom', Sir Ranolph de Brock. His name may well have been lent to this estate. Certainly by the time of Edward I, it is known that a Sir Warren de Brockhull was in residence here.

In 1498 the grand-daughter of the last of this line married a John Tournay, who took up the estate and it was the last of his successors, a William Tournay, who died in 1903 and was buried on the island in the lake.

The owner of Brockhill Park from 1911 to 1942 was Col William Tylden, whose executors sold the estate to the Kent County Council in 1947, when Brockhill Secondary School opened. The Country Park opened in 1986.

This 54 acre Country Park is open daily (except Christmas Day) from 9.00am to dusk. It contains the attractive combination of woodland, lake and streams leading to a fine valley from which views of the sea can be obtained.

There are two walks within the Park. The 'Valley Walk' is a waymarked walk which features the easiest, most scenic route around the valley at the southern end of the site. A more unusual trail found in the Country Park is 'The Badger of Brockhill', a game which involves hunting out clues around the site. A special leaflet is provided which describes this particular trail.

A countryside ranger is based at this County Park and will be pleased to answer your queries. Tel: (0303) 266327.

12 Willow Wood

Storm damage, from the hurricane of 16 October 1987, can still be seen here. Where giant trees have fallen, light has entered, encouraging the growth of flowers and tree saplings. Sycamore readily regenerates. Upturned sweet chestnut stools were previously coppiced and are again producing new growth.

13 Saltwood Rectory and American Garden

The Rectors of Saltwood (with the chapels of Hythe attached) were always prominent men appointed by the Archbishop. This culminated in the appointment in 1812 of James Croft, the Archbishop's son-in-law, who later became a Canon of Canterbury and Archdeacon, and did not die until 1869. He formed the American gardens in the extensive rectory grounds, although they were badly mutilated when the (now defunct) branch railway to Hythe was cut through the area in 1874.

14 Saltwood Church

Dedicated to St Peter and St Paul, the church has close associations with Canterbury.

Historical records of the Manor of Saltwood show that the Lady Leoflaede, widow of a Saxon Thane, gave it to the Archbishop of Canterbury. Until the 19th century all the churches in Hythe were only chapels attached to this church.

The earliest part of the present church dates from the 12th century and the remains of one of the original Norman windows of the nave (although now blocked in) can be seen on the right of the porch. The tower dates from about 1100 and originally had an unusual gable roof. The chancel was greatly enlarged in the 13th century and now contains some very fine brasses, the oldest of which is of Rector Johannes Verien, dated 1370. There is also an engraving of Thomas Brockhill and his wife, dated 1437.

WEST HYTHE BRIDGE

15 Saltwood Castle

This was the only castle belonging to the Archbishop of Canterbury, and was inhabited by various important knights who, as their Archbishop's tenants, had to guard this important area of coastline west of the great royal castle at Dover. The mid-12th-century inner curtain wall and towers still survive, as well as the ruins of 13th and 14th-century buildings (solar, hall, kitchen, and chapel), on the south side of the inner bailey. Because of the threat of invasion from France in the 1380s, a massive new gate was built on the east (similar to the contemporary Westgate in Canterbury), with a new enlarged outer bailey and gatehouse. The latter can be seen from the road beside Grange Farm.

On 20 December 1170 the four infamous knights rode from Saltwood Castle to Canterbury to murder the Archbishop Thomas à Becket, and rid King Henry of 'that turbulent priest'.

The last royal visitor was Queen Elizabeth I who dined at the castle with Sir Walter Raleigh. Shortly afterwards, in 1580, an earthquake made it uninhabitable until its restoration during this century. The castle is now the home of the Hon Alan Clark MP, elder son of the late Lord Kenneth Clark, well known for the TV series 'Civilisation'.

16 Postling Down

This small area of steep chalk downland has not been improved for agriculture and so still retains a rich natural flora. Where rabbits graze a short turf is maintained and so encourages smaller herbs to flourish. The area is rich in butterflies. To the east is an area of open access land provided by the landowner as part of the Countryside Stewardship arrangements. This scheme, which has been initiated by the Countryside Commission, offers incentives to landowners to conserve, enhance and restore some of England's most distinctive landscapes and to create opportunities for people to enjoy them through improved access.

17 Postling Church

This fine small church was built soon after the Norman Conquest and is mentioned in Domesday Book. Many of the quoin (corner) stones in the original church are made of Quarr stone from the Isle of Wight (it is characterised by the presence of thousands of

broken shells). In the 13th century the church was given to the nearby St Radegund's Abbey, and the chancel was lengthened and a small tower added. Inside there is a unique dedicatory inscription of the 12th century, as well as the cut-off ends of carved and painted timbers for the rood loft.

It is worth noting that the church, and its neighbouring manor, are situated close to where several springs, the source of the East Stour, rise at the foot of the downs.

18 Tolsford Hill

On the hilltop is a group of round Bronze Age barrows unfortunately badly damaged by bomb craters and other disturbances during the last war. The North Downs of east Kent were once covered with large numbers of these barrows, but sadly very many of them

have been destroyed in the last two centuries. The barrows were created as burial mounds between 3,500 and 4,000 years ago.

The views from the hilltop over the Elham Valley and the Channel repay the climb up to the summit.

The radio transmission station provides a communications link with the Continent and stands out at night with its glowing red beacons.

USEFUL ADDRESSES AND/OR TELEPHONE NUMBERS

If you have any comments or suggestions about this or any other recreation route, please contact the Access and Recreation Officer, Planning Department, Kent County Council, Springfield, Maidstone, Kent ME14 2LX, telephone Maidstone (0622) 696168.

The routes should not be obstructed in any way but if they are please contact the Public Rights of Way Manager, Highways and Transportation Department, Kent County Council, Springfield, Maidstone, Kent ME14 2LX, telephone (0622) 696740.

Tourist Information

Folkestone: Tourist Information Centre, Harbour Street, Folkestone, Kent CT20 1QN, telephone Folkestone (0303) 258594.

Hythe: Tourist Information Centre, Prospect Road Car Park, Hythe CT21 5NH, telephone Hythe (0303) 267799.
(NB. Not open in winter months).

Ramblers' Association, 1/5 Wandsworth Road, London SW8 2XX, telephone (071-582)

6878. Kent Area Secretary: Brian Arguile, 42 Waldron Drive, Loose, Maidstone, Kent ME15 9TH, telephone Maidstone (0622) 744207.

Countryside Commission, South East Regional Office, 4th Floor, 71 Kingsway, London WC2B 6ST, telephone (071-831) 3510.

Ordnance Survey, Romsey Road, Maybush, Southampton, Hants SO9 4DH, telephone Southampton (0703) 792000.

Weatherdial (up to date weather forecast). South Kent Coastal 0898 14 12 10

PURPLE ORCHID

OTHER WALKING OPPORTUNITIES

If you have enjoyed these walks and would like to explore other waymarked walking routes in Kent, write to the Access and Recreation Officer (listed elsewhere) for a publications price list. Other circular walk guidebooks in this series are planned and in preparation.

It is possible for you to devise your own circular walks using the extensive rights of way network throughout the county. Information about these can be obtained by studying either the Ordnance Survey Pathfinder maps or the Kent County Council Definitive Maps of Public Rights of Way. Copies of the latter can be inspected at public libraries or district council offices. In the event of difficulty please contact the Public Rights of Way Manager (listed elsewhere).

The Brockhill walks link to the Saxon Shore Way, a 140 mile linear route which traces the old shoreline between Gravesend on the Thames Estuary and Rye in East Sussex. The name comes from a series of fortifications built by the Romans to defend the country against Saxon pirate raids.

LYMPNE CASTLE

Publication:
'Saxon Shore Way Guide in ten sections' - Kent area of the Ramblers' Association, c/o Mr P Miller, 104 Hamelin Road, Darland, Gillingham, Kent ME7 3ER.

The Brockhill walks also link to the North Downs Way, one of twelve National Trails in Britain, which runs for 140 miles between Farnham in Surrey and Dover in Kent, with an alternative loop through Canterbury. The route mainly follows the ridge of the North Downs and there are fine panoramic views.

Publications:
North Downs Way National Trail Guide - Neil Curtis, Aurum Press, 10 Museum Street, London WC1A 1JS.

North Downs Way, A Users Guide - Kent County Council, Planning Department, Springfield, Maidstone, Kent ME14 2LX.

North Downs Way Walks - Kent County Council, Planning Department, Springfield, Maidstone, Kent ME14 2LX.

COUNTRYSIDE ACCESS CHARTER

YOUR RIGHTS OF WAY ARE
Public footpaths - on foot only.
Bridleways - on foot, horseback and pedal cycle.
Byways - (usually old roads), most 'roads used as public paths' and, of course, public roads - all traffic.
Use maps, signs and waymarks. Ordnance Survey Pathfinder and Landranger maps show most public rights of way.